COPPER

A TRUE BOOK®

by

Salvatore Tocci

Children's Press®
A Division of Scholastic Inc.

New York Toronto London Auckland Sydney
Mexico City New Delhi Hong Kong
Danbury, Connecticut

These plates and bracelets are made of copper.

Reading Consultant
Julia McKenzie Munemo, MEd
New York, New York

Content Consultant
John A. Benner
Austin, Texas

The photo on the cover shows copper tubing. The photo on the title page shows copper wire.

The author and the publisher are not responsible for injuries or accidents that occur during or from any experiments. Experiments should be conducted in the presence of or with the help of an adult. Any instructions of the experiments that require the use of sharp, hot, or other unsafe items should be conducted by or with the help of an adult.

Library of Congress Cataloging-in-Publication Data

Tocci, Salvatore.
Copper / by Salvatore Tocci.
    p. cm. — (A true book)
    Includes bibliographical references and index.
    ISBN 0-516-23693-8 (lib. bdg.)   0-516-25569-X (pbk.)
    1. Copper—Juvenile literature. I. Title. II. Series.
QD181.C9T63 2005
669.3—dc22   2004013149

CHILDREN'S PRESS, and A TRUE BOOK™, and associated logos are trademarks and or registered trademarks of Scholastic Library Publishing. SCHOLASTIC and associated logos are trademarks and or registered trademarks of Scholastic Inc.
7 8 9 10 R 14 13 12 11 10 09   62

Contents

This 1943 penny is
95 percent copper.

How Much Is It Worth?

Do you collect anything?
Many people collect coins.
Each year, the U.S. government makes billions of coins.
Since 1787, the U.S. government has made more than
300 billion pennies alone. For
the most part, these pennies
are worth no more than their

face value—one cent. However, some of these one-cent coins are worth much more. One example is a penny that was made in 1943.

At that time, the United States was involved in World War II. Before the war, the government used copper metal to make pennies. In 1943, however, all the available copper was needed for the war effort. As a result, the government stopped using copper and started using other metals to make pennies.

While making the switch, someone forgot to replace all of the copper in the machinery used to make pennies. About forty copper pennies were made in 1943 and found their way into circulation. They soon became very valuable. In 1958, one of these copper pennies sold for $40,000.

Today's penny is only 2.5 percent copper.

In 1996, another 1943 copper penny sold for $82,500.

If you collect coins, perhaps you have a 1943 copper penny that may be worth as much as $100,000 today. If you do find one, check it closely. Many fake 1943 copper pennies have been made. To find out if yours is real, all you have to do is learn a few things about copper.

What Is Copper?

Copper is an element. An **element** is the building block of matter. **Matter** is the stuff or material that makes up everything in the universe. This book, the chair you are sitting on, and even you are made of matter.

There are millions of different kinds of matter. However, there are just a few more than one hundred different elements. How can so many different kinds of matter be made up of so few elements? Think about the English language. Just twenty-six letters can be arranged to make up all the words in the English language. Likewise, the one hundred or so different

Copper is found in several minerals, such as this piece of malachite, that American Indians use to make jewelry.

elements can be arranged to make up all the kinds of matter in the universe.

Every element has a name and a symbol. The symbol for copper is Cu. This symbol comes from the Latin word *cuprum*, the name given by the early Romans to the Mediterranean island we now call Cyprus. This island was one of the most important sources of copper for the Roman Empire. However, the history of copper usage goes back even farther in time. Copper beads found in Iraq have been reported to be some eleven thousand years old. Exactly where and when copper was first used by humans is not known.

Copper, like most of the other elements, is a metal. A metal is any substance that is a good **conductor** of electricity. The ability to conduct electricity is the only feature all metals have in common.

However, some metals conduct electricity better than others. For example, copper conducts electricity about six times better than the metal iron.

There are other features that many, but not all, metals share. For example, many metals are magnetic, which means they are attracted to a magnet.

Attracting Metals

Collect an assortment of metal objects, such as a piece of copper wire, a steel washer, an iron nail, a brass screw, aluminum foil, and a variety of coins. Hold a magnet close to each object. Which metal objects are attracted to the magnet? Coins today are made mostly of a metal called zinc. A magnet attracts zinc, so your coins should have been attracted to the magnet. Copper, however, is not attracted to a magnet. If you were lucky enough to have a 1943 copper penny among your coins, it should not have been attracted to the magnet.

Unlike many metals, copper is not magnetic. However, copper does have other features that are shared by many metals. For example, copper is an excellent conductor of heat. Copper is also **malleable**. This means copper can be pounded into different shapes without breaking. Copper is also **ductile**. This means copper can be drawn into a wire or pounded into a thin sheet.

Copper metal has a red-orange color.

Copper wire is used to wire homes for electricity.

Some metals are very reactive. This means they combine with other elements easily. Sometimes, they do so quite violently. For example, the metal sodium causes an explosion when it is dropped into water.

In contrast, copper does not combine easily or quickly with other elements. However, copper does combine very slowly with other elements, such as the oxygen in the air.

The patina coating protects the copper skin of the Statue of Liberty from corrosion.

Two elements combine to form a **compound**. The compound that copper and oxygen form has a blue-green color and is called patina.

Pure copper is found only in small amounts in Earth. Most copper must be extracted from compounds or ores taken from mines. A major source of copper is an ore called chalcopyrite. This ore is commonly known as "fool's gold" because the

Most copper in use today was extracted from mines like the one shown here.

specks of copper fool people into thinking it is gold.

Extracting copper from an ore involves several steps: grinding the ore into a fine powder, heating it in a furnace, and passing an electric current through it. The copper extracted from ores can then be used for various purposes.

How Is Copper Useful?

About half the copper extracted from ores is used to make electrical wiring and equipment. At one time, aluminum, another metal element, was used in electrical wiring for new homes. However, copper has replaced aluminum for home wiring, mainly because copper conducts electricity better. Copper can also be twisted and stretched with less chance of breaking.

Copper is also used in plumbing because it does not corrode when it gets wet. Copper's ability to conduct heat makes it useful in other ways. For example, copper coils are used in refrigerators, air conditioners, and dehumidifiers. The use of these copper coils allows

Because they conduct heat well, copper pots are used for cooking.

refrigerators to keep foods fresh, air conditioners to keep homes cool, and dehumidifiers to keep basements dry.

Copper also plays an important role inside the human body. A very small amount of copper is needed to maintain good health. A substance the body needs in a tiny amount to maintain good health is called a **micronutrient**. Copper is a micronutrient. The recommended daily requirement of copper is 1–2 milligrams for an adult and 0.5–1 mg for a child younger than ten years. This amount of copper is found in a balanced diet.

Copper is used to keep blood vessels elastic so that blood flows smoothly. Copper is also used to make collagen, a substance that keeps skin looking healthy and bones strong. Without copper, the immune system would not work as well to fight germs and prevent infections. In addition, copper helps the nervous system, including the brain, function properly.

Other animals also need copper to stay healthy. An interesting example is the horseshoe crab. This animal uses copper to make a substance that carries oxygen in its blood. However, this

The blood of a horseshoe crab is blue because of the copper it contains.

substance makes a horseshoe crab's blood look blue rather than the red color we normally associate with blood.

Compounds that contain copper are also widely used. In fact, the use of copper compounds has a long history. The ancient Egyptians used a copper compound to dye their clothing. This compound prevented the dye from washing or fading away. More than five thousand years later, this copper compound is still being used for the same purpose.

One of the most common uses of copper compounds is

in agriculture. This use of copper was the result of an unusual observation made by a scientist. During the 1880s, a French scientist noticed that certain grapevines were less likely to develop plant diseases. These vines were growing near roads, where anyone passing by could pick the grapes. The farmers had sprayed the grapes with a copper compound, which made the grapes look unappealing. This way, people passing by were not as likely to pick the grapes and eat them. What the farmers did not realize was that the copper compound also protected their grapes against diseases. Today, this same copper compound is applied to all kinds of crops throughout the world to prevent plant diseases.

What Is a Copper Alloy?

Until 1837, all pennies made by the U.S. government were pure copper. After then, pennies were only 95 percent copper, except for those made in 1943. Starting in 1982, less copper was used because the copper cost more than the coin was worth. Today, a penny contains

Brass is used to make things like instruments and buttons.

only 2.5 percent copper. The
rest of the coin is zinc metal.
Together, copper and zinc make
up an **alloy** known as brass.

Cleaning Brass

Add a quarter cup (60 milliliters) of white vinegar and 1 teaspoon (5 ml) of salt to a clear glass bowl. Stir until the salt dissolves in the vinegar. Place several dirty pennies in the bowl. After five minutes, take out the pennies. Rinse them well with running water and then place them on a paper towel to dry. The pennies should sparkle. The vinegar and salt removed the copper compound on the surface of the coins that made them look dirty. Try using soda, juice, and milk to see if any of them work with salt to clean brass pennies.

Brass was used to make the shells for the explosives fired by these World War II artillery guns.

Brass is used for a variety of purposes. During World War II, some of the copper that would have been used to make pennies was instead used to make brass. In turn, the brass was used to make various items needed for the war. These items included artillery shells and buttons for officers' uniforms. Today, brass is used to make faucets, musical instruments, lamps, door handles, locks, hinges, and screws.

Bronze is another copper alloy. Bronze is made by mixing copper with tin. Bronze is mainly used for creating outdoor sculptures and for making hardware for doors, windows, and furniture.

The use of bronze has a long history. Bronze objects first appeared about four thousand years ago at the start of a time period known as the Bronze Age. During that time, people used bronze to make jewelry, weapons, and household items, such as drinking cups and razors. Bronze was also used to make coins. Unlike a 1943 U.S. copper penny, an ancient Roman bronze coin can be bought today for only a few dollars.

Fun Facts About Copper

- The torch on the Statue of Liberty was never lit with a real flame. Rather, the flame is made by the sun or by floodlights shining on a sheet of copper covered with a thin layer of gold.

- The most valuable U.S. copper coin, known as the No Pole half cent, made in 1796, was sold in 1996 for $506,000.

- The term "brass band" is derived from the musical instruments made from this alloy, including trombones, tubas, and trumpets.

- The term "Army brass" is derived from the buttons on the officers' uniforms.

- Silver is the only metal that conducts electricity better than copper does.

- Brass and bronze do not conduct electricity as well as pure copper does.

- A copper bar 4 inches (10 centimeters) thick can be heated, rolled, and then drawn into a round wire that is thinner than a human hair. This wire is twenty million times longer than the original bar.

To Find Out More

If you would like to learn more about copper, check out these additional resources.

 **Books**

Clegg, Helen, and Mary Larom. **Making Wire Jewelry: 60 Easy Projects in Silver, Copper & Brass.** Sterling Publishing, 1999.

Llewellyn, Claire. **Metal.** Franklin Watts, 2002.

United States Copper Coins. Bowers & Merena Galleries, 1984.

☀️ Organizations and Online Sites

Copper in Your Home
http://www.copper.org/ copperhome/copperandkids _home.html

Read about the history of copper, which was the only metal known to prehistoric humans for nearly five thousand years. You can also click on links that will take you to information about how copper was used to restore the Statue of Liberty and how copper is extracted from ores.

A Green Potato
http://www.phys.virginia. edu/classes/620/electricity _activities.html#potato

Use two pennies and a battery to pass electricity through a potato. A greenish color will start to appear around one of the pennies. This site will explain what this greenish copper compound is.

Indian Head Cent
http://www.ustreas.gov/ education/fact-sheets/ currency/indian-head.html

This site discusses the Indian Head cent that was produced by the U.S. Mint from 1859 through 1909. Some of these coins were made of 88 percent copper. However, none of these coins is nearly as valuable as the 1943 copper penny because almost two billion Indian Head cents were made.

Copper Caper
http://www.exploratorium. edu/science_explorer/ copper_caper.html

Carry out an experiment in which you can coat a nail and screw with copper.

45

Important Words

alloy substance made by mixing two or more metals that retain their individual properties

compound substance formed when two or more elements are joined

conductor substance through which electricity or heat passes

ductile capable of being drawn into a wire or pounded into a thin sheet

element building block of matter

malleable capable of being pounded into various shapes without breaking

matter stuff or material that makes up everything in the universe

micronutrient substance that a living thing needs in tiny amounts to keep healthy

Index

Meet the Author

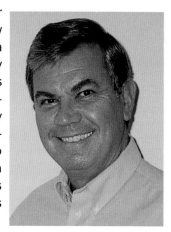

Salvatore Tocci is a science writer who lives in East Hampton, New York, with his wife Patti. He was a high school biology and chemistry teacher for almost thirty years. His books include a high school chemistry textbook and an elementary school series that encourages students to perform experiments to learn about science. The paint on the hull of his sailboat contains copper, which keeps barnacles from attaching to the boat.